MY KILL ADORE HIM

THE ANDRÉS MONTOYA POETRY PRIZE

2004, *Pity the Drowned Horses*, Sheryl Luna
Final Judge: Robert Vasquez

2006, *The Outer Bands*, Gabriel Gomez
Final Judge: Valerie Martínez

2008, *My Kill Adore Him*, Paul Martínez Pompa
Final Judge: Martín Espada

The Andrés Montoya Poetry Prize, named after the late California native

and author of the award-winning book, *The Iceworker Sings*,

supports the publication of a first book by a Latino or Latina poet.

Awarded every other year, the prize is administered by Letras Latinas—

the literary program of the Institute for Latino Studies

at the University of Notre Dame

MY KILL ADORE HIM

PAUL MARTÍNEZ POMPA

University of Notre Dame Press

Notre Dame, Indiana

Library of Congress Cataloging-in-Publication Data

Martínez Pompa, Paul.

My kill adore him / Paul Martínez Pompa.

p.   cm. — (Andrés Montoya poetry prize)

ISBN-13: 978-0-268-03518-1 (pbk. : alk. paper)

ISBN-10: 0-268-03518-0 (pbk. : alk. paper)

1. Political poetry, American.   I. Title.

PS3613.A7869M9   2009

813'.6—dc22

2009022899

for Mom & Dad

and

for my sisters

CONTENTS

II. CITY OF BROKEN

III. THE WAR ON POETS GOES ON

ACKNOWLEDGMENTS

Grateful acknowledgement is made to the following publications in which some of these poems appeared, sometimes in earlier versions:

After Hours: A Journal of Chicago Writing and Art: "Flirting"

Barrow Street: part four of "Mykilladoreher"

Borderlands: Texas Poetry Review: "While Late Capitalism"

Epicenter: "On the Significance of Che, Dead in the Laundry House of the Vallegrande Hospital, Nuestro Señor de Malta"

Free Lunch: "The War on Poets Goes On"

Indiana English: "The Performer"

LOCUSPOINT: "The Body as Weapon, as Inspiration"

Michigan Avenue Review: "Garbage Truck"

Palabra: "Drink Bovicola"

Rhino: "Police Dog," "Want"

"Commercial Break" appeared in *Telling Tongues: A Latin@ Anthology on Language Experience*, edited by Louis Gerard Mendoza and Toni Nelson Herrera (National City, Califas: Calaca Press, 2007).

"Retablos: 10 Deleted Tongues" appeared in a broadside series created by Roberto Harrison.

Several poems here appeared in the chapbook *Pepper Spray* (Momotombo Press, 2006).

Nine poems here, some under different titles, also appeared in *The Wind Shifts: New Latino Poetry*, edited by Francisco Aragón (Tucson: University of Arizona Press, 2007).

INTRODUCTION TO THE POEMS

This is one tough, smart poet. The poems of Paul Martínez Pompa are gritty and visceral, but never cross the line into sensationalism. They are poems that vividly evoke the urban world, especially Chicago, without ever lapsing into urban cliché. They are poems that seek justice for the Latino community without ever resorting to the overheated language that all too often consigns poetry of social conscience to oblivion. Martínez Pompa is a poet of the image, a poet of strong diction, a poet of meticulous craft. He puts that craft at the service of los olvidados, the forgotten ones: the usual suspects brutalized by police, factory workers poisoned by their environment, the victim of a homophobic beating in the boys' bathroom. Yet this poet's keen eye, sense of humor and gift for irony help these poems to rise above the wreckage of their circumstances. Nowhere else will you find a poem celebrating a Mexican grandmother's phone call to the local Pizza Hut. Martínez Pompa's observation of a garbage truck may remind us of Williams and his poem about a fire engine; his compassion for the damned may bring Whitman or Hughes to mind. Paul Martínez Pompa, however, is very much his own man and his own poet, independent and honest. His is a unique voice, speaking the truth with clarity. Welcome.

—Martín Espada,
Judge

MY KILL ADORE HIM

As hypotheticals go, "man" seems to me the most damaging.

—Joe Wenderoth

I

A LESSON IN MASCULINITY

FILM STRIP

We've been isolated from the girls
to learn our bodies. Our desks harder
than our hairless asses. They shudder
beneath us when Mr. Griffey fingers

the 16mm reel. He mumbles directions
to himself, orders Danny S. to pull
down the white screen. We swell
into concentration as grainy scenes

flicker past our heads. The projector's
clatter surrounds us like criminals:
narrated cross-section of the testicles,
the animated penis a cruel reminder

of our fathers. Strange men we've seen
through cracked doors. Their nude
bodies a revelation, a portrait of manhood
larger than anything we could imagine.

THE PERFORMER

I play it chingon in full length
mirrors. Mad doggin' my reflection—
some kind of *don't fuck with me*
skin language. Rollin' hard on
suburban boulevards. Scare

the white off kids, teachers shake
their heads. Almost beggin' for a beat
down. Toy gun real enough
to fear. Step to the mirror, pull out my
what-chu gonna do now?

Pray he backs down, punks out.
Everyone watchin', the gun
trembles in the mirror. Pistol whip.
He goes down. All the kids cheer
my head thick with e — g — o.

PULLING TONGUE

Lissette opens me with her fingers.
    I struggle to breathe
with her tongue in my mouth.
    Suddenly we are stars

in a Mexi-Rican romance film
    that unravels on her aunt's stoop.
Backlit by the flickering streetlamp
    an audience of boys forms

and I feel the pressure to comply.
    Catcalls & uneasy laughter,
I kiss harder. My finger stutters
    over her knee, her thigh—

You fuckin Mexicans kiss like girls
    as she slaps my arm,
the crash of the metal storm
    door behind her. The boys

swell into a mob set to detonate
    the entire block. I rise
& brace myself for their eyes,
    their bodies that wet the night.

THE PHYSICS OF CRIME

With Popsicles shoved down our pants
we imagine an entire police squadron
assembled outside, ready to pounce.
The aisles blur and we search each other's

eyes for something we won't dare name.
We'll make it out alive but in eight years
you'll spill from a motorcycle at 130 mph
fleeing men in cruisers hungry for death.

I'll have just enrolled in junior college
hidden like a fugitive behind books,
learning to steal the stories of strangers
& friends. I now struggle to write

our giddy walk home after the heist.
Only recall how we slid past the cashier.
Our genitals numb, our fists tight enough
to squeeze the breath from someone.

EDWIN SUCKS DICK

First in the boy's bathroom,
middle stall, where no kid dared

poop for fear of having the door
kicked in. Then it was scribbled

on his gym locker. Capital letters
& crooked penis to illustrate.

Sometimes it was shouted
from groups of boys he passed in the hall.

It got physical once as he stripped
off sweaty gym shorts. A clumsy

first swing grazed his cheek. He
took another perfectly to his mouth.

One by one more boys jumped in.
Others just watched—afraid, aroused.

OFFICER FRIENDLY

Me & Z walking the block when a cop shoots
his spotlight in our eyes when 2 more police roll
up with guns & fear & get on the fuckin ground
I do but Z moves too slow & the sidewalk don't budge
when they drive his face into it a cop fumbles
his cuffs lowers his gun says wait that's not the guy
sorry amigo & they flee.

THE PEANUT BUTTER & JELLY NARRATIVES

When I was ten, my older sister walked in on us—me, the dog, the peanut butter smeared you know where. She yelled at us to stop, said she was gonna tell Mom. All evening I lay awake waiting for her to come home from work.

———

Since I never spoke in 1st grade, my teacher sat me with the Mexicanos during lunch. She said I'd be more comfortable there. Every day Ruben with his tortilla & beans. Every day Lupita with her tortilla & rice. Every day me with my peanut butter & jelly. Every day we ate in silence, staring at each other's food.

———

At twelve I tore crust from a jelly sandwich to lure a stray beagle into the garage. I held the crust close to his nose, pulling away each time he poked or barked at my fist. I told him shut up, let him lick my knuckles & fingers.

FLIRTING

In 5th grade I told Griselda Lopez
she had a face like a brick. Her hair
spilled onto my desk and I'd tug
to see how hard I could pull before
she'd feel it. Sometimes she nudged
her desk forward not bothering
to slap or call me *pendejo* anymore.
Then I'd turn to Bryan Massey.
Gum wrapper, spit ball, whatever
was on hand I'd lob at his head
and he'd finger-flick it back. I hit
Jill Pickford on purpose once.
Stupid Meck-sah-kin. She spit it
like a curse or stiff punch to my gut.
I don't know if I hated her for being
white or for making me hate being
Mexican. On family-tree day
we all stood before the world
map to tell where our relatives lived.
When I pointed to Illinois, Jill yelled
No, you're from down there. Down there.
I felt a fire in my skin as all the kids
laughed. All except Griselda
who sat at her desk. Stone faced.

A LESSON IN MASCULINITY

She taught me to wipe
the urine dribble
off the tip
until Papi said no—
men don't wipe
they shake.

BLOW BY BLOW

       he enters the room. & his father. pretends
not to notice. together they watch heavyweights. pour

       their bodies into the ring. he learns. it is nothing
to pummel a man's face. as long as you embrace him

       immediately after. this is how they bond.
the television as conversation. how to talk with your fists.

       when he's older he won't. feel. his father's language.
he will not collapse. when the words touch his. body.

       he will drop only after finding. his father
alone with the television. talking. talking. talking.

WITH THE EYES ALONE

The air is like gunmetal.
                                An explosion
of bass rattles a Nissan's trunk as it waits

the stoplight. I cross the street
and my breath rises
                                blends into the night

like a car alarm.
                                A man clutches frozen
towels & tip box outside CITGO's carwash.

His face: scarf-smothered
                                ninja-style
as if seeing & breathing were done

with the eyes alone.
                                The clerk inside looks
vulnerable till I spot mounted cameras.

What else—baseball bat? Pistol?
Something defensive
                                deadly

tucked under the register.
                                I continue
home in skin not safe to be at night.

II

CITY OF BROKEN

CLAMOR

the bus fills & empties like an aluminum lung. what he says
I lose. in the clamor of. gears. bodies. words

obsolete when you see how. she breathes him. how he is
draped in the orchestra of her. fingers. untouched

by this. city of broken lovers who slip across
the bus window. no I cannot hear what he mouths.

I watch the clamor. youth & desire fleeing
their seats. remember when we were young. bold

enough to love that hard. trust was our eyes. closed.
our mouths undoing each other's. bodies. I'm exposed

when he catches me. eyes set to cut. how he softens
when she cups his cheek. turns it back. to her.

WANT

July smothers the city like a drunk
lover and the shade offers nothing
but an illusion of cool. A cluster

of sun-whipped men leans on brick
that looks more chewed up steak
than wall. They want work

and wait here in the hot for an offer.
One man wipes sweat from above
his lip. Another moves slow

as tar softening over this
Home Depot lot. An extended cab
truck drives past, stops—waves

of heat rise from the hood. The window
rolls down and an arm extends out,
thrusting two fingers into the air.

After two men climb onto the bed
like spent athletes, the truck pulls
away. A man left behind tilts

his head up as if ready for the sky
to burst & soil everything
with water.

HOW TO HEAR CHICAGO

Here a spirit must yell
to be heard yet a bullet

need only whisper to make
its point—sometimes I imagine

you right before your death
with an entire city in your ears.

RECOIL

After the bullets, the sidewalk breaks

under the sun's indifference. Mothers fall

numb as photographs & candle wax

drape the corner. No one saw the recoil

of flesh but the memory of lead cuts

through the crowd like a mirror. Cop eyes

blur into the night watching liquor store

security video from across the street.

This chore of solving like trying to piece

together a jigsaw puzzle, skin-side down.

POLICE DOG

it's all just
play   to wrap

your mouth
around a man's

wrist   barely
break skin

to growl   tug
hold on till

the officers
arrive   only then

do things
get serious

THE DEBRIS IT CARRIES

Outside the window, the rain
   taps the sidewalk and I realize
I could sit & watch this forever.
   The weeds are reassuring,
how thousands will rise
   from something fallen.
I can't write about you directly
   so I write the water flowing
curbside, the debris it carries to vanish
   below ground. Our last conversation
a poem I cannot revise, a spill
   that left the bed littered with words
unsaid. I envy this bird that searches
   the grass knowing only what is necessary
to survive. Envy more that place
   where the rain begins its descent
as if distance could make the heart grow
   dumber.

MEN WATCHING MEN
(El Gato Negro Bar)

I'm not drunk
enough so I order one
more bottle. He shoves
a lime down its throat
& I see myself

surrounded by men
who watch the night
in a mirror
behind the bar.
We smoke

our cigarettes
with purpose, pretending
courage is something
we can suck in.
Click of the jukebox

& the treble
cuts the air. A man
holds his woman
tight enough to feel her
penis press his belly.

Dance floor strobe light
captures their bodies.
Her cheek on his
shoulder, her breath
on our necks.

BONES

Your feet are a slow train
wreck of cuneiforms
                    & metatarsals fallen off

track. Too many shifts
standing, bagging melon & meat
                    frozen peas & six-packs wedged

careful against egg cartons
loaves of bread
                    tomatoes that piss if touched

too hard. At home you stand
at a sink full of yesterday's
                    plates, sauce-caked pots

butter knives tough
with peanut butter.
                    Nights you fall

asleep on the couch, trying to ignore
the 52 bones of your feet
                    each one humming its own pain.

GARBAGE TRUCK

After it lifts the army-green, stuffed
dumpster over its head and the trash
falls to the receptacle, it hulks
backward with a cadenced beep as if
to say, get out the fucking way, please.

HIT & RUN

To the medics he is nothing
but a homeless wound, breathing

litter flung to the street
like a half-smoked cigarette

that slowly wills itself out.
Fire-truck sirens on mute,

the spectacle now the shaken witness.
Her story unfolds in sentence

fragments & hand gestures. Two cops
direct traffic, another swaps

notes with a detective whose joke
cracks the stiff veneer. Cars choke

the intersection, their horns begin to spit:
Let's go, we aint got time for this shit.

ELEGY FOR WINTER

All night the plows pummeled the streets
with salt and sidewalks disappeared
under snow. Folding chairs & milk crates
mark the exhumation sites of unburied

cars. Each block is a struggle. Bungalows
eclipsed by huddled three-flats. Trendy
lofts rise from hyperbolic potholes
large enough to swallow the entire city.

We will forget all this by spring
when the snow has returned to the sky
and the streets are bound with nothing
but tar. Now the gray

ice hangs like murder from the trees.
This looming we nearly mistake for beauty.

SIEVE

i am searching for a way. to fall
into your skin. to erase. what grows
under. your hospital bed a home
away from. memory. the vanishing act
who fathered your children. how to reconstruct
the ruins. no fist small enough. to unravel this
knot in my chest. as if i could. heal. how easy
he is to hate. a wound. in a wound
labeled your body. a diagnosis on a slip
of paper. not a story. the empty space
i too have colonized. forgive my desire
to pour you. through me. embrace
the damaged parts. i am searching for
a way to fall. a way to bleed. him. me.

III

THE WAR ON POETS GOES ON

RETABLOS: 10 DELETED TONGUES

Oh-no—
Watch out for the Mexican
-American border patrol
officer. He's fluent in badge
gun & pepper
spray.

Doze—
Hiss-panics panic when I step
to the mic to spit Chicano shit.

Trace—
If I stand on this side of the Big River
& you stand on that side,
I can't see you unless you talk real
loud.

Cutthroat—
(The writer intended to convey _____ here,
but due to the limitations of the writer's language . . .)

Sea-gold—
That language does not make cents.
When that language makes cents, I will invest in it. Emotionally.

Says—
My son goes to college. I'm very proud of him.
Now he's a comunista and I don't understand
a pinche word he says.

See-it-think—
My father. 9-years-old. At the blackboard.
I will not speak Spanish in class.
I will not speak Spanish in class.
I will not speak . . .

Ouch-woe—
my pocho   tongue loss   a second language   me
with a Spanish   last name who   can't talk
Spanish.

New-wavy—
Whisper something sexy & dirty
in my ear, something Mexican.

Deist—
Since Jesus never learned
English, he was promptly denied
a second coming
into Arizona.

THE WAR ON POETS GOES ON

(O'Hare International Airport)

I didn't get past security
without them sweatin'
my trendy carry-on, loaded

with a two-pound brick
of chapbooks, wrapped
like contraband

or a cheap Christmas gift.
Unwrap it
he said & I tore it

open like a manchild
desperate for nothing
but attention, half fearing

half wanting a Gestapo
bumrush to drag me off,
lock me in a dark room.

That's right, man, you got me
on possession with intent
to distribute. I'm flyin'

to New York with reified
revolution in my bag.
Haul me in, deem me

enemy combatant, one poem
alone could wipe out
an entire city block.

But he didn't even flinch
when he saw my books.
All I got was

we can't let anything
dangerous on, these are fine,
go on through, enjoy your trip.

SUCKER MC

your poem wind
milling double clutch
tween the legs can't sink
a fuckin free throw

ON THE SIGNIFICANCE OF CHE, DEAD IN THE LAUNDRY HOUSE OF THE VALLEGRANDE HOSPITAL, NUESTRO SEÑOR DE MALTA

In the photo your corpse is draped over
a wash basin as Bolivian soldiers stare

and poke, careful not to get too close
to your sunken chest. Your Jesus

veneer tempts the nuns to clip a lock
of hair before an agent is ordered to take

a saw to your wrists. Fingers to fall
like bullets into formaldehyde. The tale

of your body varies with each voyeur's
attempt to write it. The photo blurs

& I realize I cannot revise an icon
permanently cast as mere decoration.

Let near poets dismiss you as ironic trend,
I have nothing to say not already said.

THE BODY AS WEAPON,
AS INSPIRATION

The body as weapon, as inspiration
when she walks into a Jerusalem market
and explodes herself. Not so much
the explosive force, but the shrapnel

a year ago that tore through her
mother's chest and maimed her
brother's legs. Her father was spared
unnecessary pain—instantly dead under

the collapse of ceiling joists & plywood.
Somehow she survived. Now only a scar
on her forehead and an unofficial apology
from the State. Soon men will fall

to the ground with ringing in their ears.
There will be tiny fragments of glass
& bone caught in the skin of the undead.
There will be retaliation strikes,

missile bombardments, another round
of bulldozers. And there will be a poet
thousands of miles away, excited
by the burden of writing this   thing.

AMPUTEE ETCETERA

Nothing cuter
than a war amputee.
His limb not as fleshy ruin
but as fresh bouquet
of soft tissue, blasted with love
through desert air.

Nothing prettier
than a deserted semi-trailer
loaded with dead Mexicans.
How their mouths fall
open like little brown orchids
thirsty for a breath
of hot air.

Nothing lovelier
than a Chi-town cop
who pummels a bartender
one-third his size.
See his fists not as mallets
but as opportunity, knocking
her body again, again.

Nothing sweeter
than a white politician
who plays the erase card
when a black man speaks.
Like the weather,
cultural imperialism
gives us something
to look forward to.

Nothing truer
than a poet who resists
on paper. Admire his nerve
to condemn from a safe
distance, where he can
keep his shoes
and his conscience
perfectly clean.

THE ABUELITA POEM

I. SKIN & CORN

Her brown skin glistens as the sun
pours through the kitchen window
like gold *leche*. After grinding
the <u>*nixtamal*</u>, a word so beautifully ethnic
it must not only be italicized but underlined
to let you, the reader, know you've encountered
something beautifully ethnic, she kneads
with the hands of centuries-old ancestor
spirits who magically yet realistically posses her
until the *masa* is smooth as a *lowrider's*
chrome bumper. And I know she must do this
with care because it says so on a website
that explains how to make homemade corn *tortillas*.
So much labor for this peasant bread,
this edible art birthed from *Abuelita's*
brown skin, which is still glistening
in the sun.

II. APOLOGY

Before she died I called my abuelita
grandma. I cannot remember
if she made corn tortillas from scratch
but, O, how she'd flip the factory fresh
El Milagros (Quality Since 1950)
on the burner, bathe them in butter
& salt for her grandchildren.
How she'd knead the buttons
on the telephone, order me food
from Pizza Hut. I assure you,
gentle reader, this was done
with the spirit of Mesoamérica
ablaze in her fingertips.

POETRY READING
AT THE CAFÉ TAMALE

Not only have I disappointed the high school Spanish teacher
   who promised her students an authentic cultural experience,
the owner, I suspect, regrets the idea to feature poets
   at this four-dollar-a-tamale, suburban-strip-mall enterprise.
I begin as talking artifact but after two or three poems
   I become New-York-City-manufactured-salsa (get a rope).
I am authentic as the Diego Rivera prints nailed to the wall.

   Obligatory applause & one student is determined to ask
questions, which come in carefully rehearsed Spanish.
   Suddenly I'm back in high school, lightheaded with shame
as a white teacher interrogates me with charges I cannot answer.
   ¿Eres mexicano, verdad? sí. *¿Cien por ciento?* sí.
¿Por qué no hablas español? i don't know . . .
   Back & forth stammer between colonial tongues
& finally it's over. The owner thanks me for coming & I nod
   at his remark that selling tamales is like writing poetry.
The art of it all. Maybe the poems could be a bit more pretty,
   tú sabes, more mexicano, he explains. More polite nodding
as I swallow my wages: broccoli-stuffed tamales,
   Snapple iced-tea, stale tortilla chips in a plastic basket.

EXCLAMATION POINT

Exclamation Point—a punctuation mark that indicates strong feeling in connection with what is being said. It serves as a signpost to a reader that a sentence expresses intense feeling. An exclamation point may end a declaratory statement (Put your fuckin hands up!), a question (Do you want me to put a cap in your mexakin ass!), or a fragment (Now asshole!). It may express an exclamation (Your ass is going to jail!), a wish (If you move, I'll shoot your fuckin ass!), or a cry (Okay, okay, take it easy, officer!). As these examples show, exclamation points are commonest in written dialogue. They should be used carefully in any writing and very seldom in formal writing.

COMMERCIAL BREAK

Are your images inefficient? Is your diction bland? Are you tired of writing poetry that simply does not work? If you answered *yes* to any of these questions, consider what a Mexican can do for you. Strategically placed, a Mexican will stimulate and fire up your drab, white poem.

Here at Pretty White Poetry, we have an inventory of Mexicans in all shades of brown. Need an authentic-indigenous tone? Try our mud-brown, Indian Mexican. Your audience will taste the lust in Montezuma's loins as they devour your lines. Want a little spice but not too much pepper? A pale-brown, Spanish concentrated Mexican is the perfect touch.

Maria, tortilla, mango, trabajo—just a sample of the hundreds of exotic words on sale waiting to decorate your verse. Even Hispanic poets sprinkle our Latin Lingo into their writing. If our selection brings authenticity to their work, imagine what it can do for yours! Just listen to what happens to the following image after being pumped with a little *Español:*

Standard Stanza:	Supercharged with Cultura:
Grandma at the stove,	*Abuelita* at the *comal,*
her skin shiny. The wind	her skin like *café con leche.*
pulls bacon & eggs	The wind pulls *huevos*
to my nose as I enter	*con chorizo* to my nose
the house.	as I enter the *casita.*

Pretty White Poetry understands the difficulty of crafting well-paced, rhythmic lines. So we've imported Salsa-smooth Puerto Rican vernacular* to make your diction dance and your syntax sway. Don't worry about mixing Mexican and Puerto Rican imagery—most of your readers won't know the difference!

Trouble with line breaks? Our Mexicans specialize in knowing exactly where it's safe to break a line. After all, that's how they get into the country in the first place!

Pretty White Poetry deals exclusively with docile, safe language. Our words are edgy, but never make liberal white readers uncomfortable—that means more publishing opportunities for you! And our Mexicans are cheap but always high quality. For here at PWP, our motto is: "If your poem has Mexicans, you know it's gonna work!"

(*Puerto Rican vernacular available only while supplies last.)

IV

WHILE LATE CAPITALISM

SHOWER STALL BALLER

(for Tim Hardaway)

Maybe Zo was hung like a six-ten stallion
but did Manute Bol's seven feet, seven

inches of sweat glistened man-swagger
penetrate the Golden State locker

room like a jungle-fevered white woman's
long, exotic fantasy? What should a man

do crammed inside a shower stall
of muscle & lather minutes after a brutal

game of half-court picks, determined elbows,
bruised flesh below a rim that swallows

then shits a leather rock to the hard wood,
to the hyperbolically large hands of gods

whose aggression is marketed to inspire
us? Check the stats: 12-man roster,

14 years in the league, 82 games each
means 12,628 exposures to NBA dick.

So it's better you fled Miami before Shaq
came with enough girth & length to make

something recoil, deep inside your jock
like an upside down question mark.

ERECTILE MISS

How dare you
dis my erectile

dysfunction.
It's much too hard

to maintain
this cheap word play

-er when Donald's trumped
up the entire cityscape.

The problem is
my head, ya prick,

these loins aren't on
fire. My boners

ship from Canada
in a child-resistant

vial but have you seen
what happens

to chorizo
once it's cooked?

MALE PATTERN

Off with your fashion
dread. This plug line is real
estate. Just try to rip off
my error dome, my dollar
dollar bills   y'all.

DRINK BOVICOLA

A well-milked patty
cake of foot rot & mastitis is

my kind of mammy gland.
That cow's a real downer but

I beat my meat any way. Slap
the Kraft on the shaft. Heinz

them hides to capitalize before & after
taste. Through hoof n mouth

we'll scarf it down & be happy
meals.

BANANA REPUBLIC POLITICK

Damn these stacks of argyle I can't have
just one merino wool V-neck beauty
on my shelves & shoulders fitted cotton crew
I bought more & saved these pretty white boys
are irresistibly high cheek bones my fantasy
factory on display as salespeople who know
what I need is more boot cut slim fit French
cuff stretch my BR card till no more poplin
fits my need-gene inseam button fly
straight leg indigo relaxed light brain
wash.

IDENTITY POLITICK

Why make my own identity when I can buy
dungarees mass produced like desire
is a predetermined trend I never buck
a system that says my denim is in
distress the working class mass surrenders
its fashion capital to a laborer who works
the look without the effort the sweat
the dinero go into holes the fray
the wash what make me
an individual.

POLITICAL PLASMA

Convenient to forget my political shtick
with a 63-inch plasma hung over
my head an empty space on the wall
plugged with what you wish you had
subwoofers beefcake as mine a gargantuan
shindig of channels a distraction in
surround sound speaks so I don't have to
waive my right to rent appliance art I boost
my lackluster libido with a dream
machine that is always turned on.

MANIFESTO

A spectre is haunting the suburbs: the spectre of illegal aliens. All the powers of suburbia—including Republican jingoists, village trustees, and a few Hispanics suffering an identity crisis—have entered into a holy alliance to rid this spectre. Now it is time that illegals openly in the face of the gringos publish their views, their aims, their tendencies, and meet this nursery tale of the spectre of illegal aliens with a manifesto of the party itself.

Illegals of all nationalities have stormed the border to sketch the following:

I.

Yes, it is true—cuando hablamos español we are talking about you. How to lower your property values. How to raise your car insurance premiums. How to steal your children, drag them across the border and sniff them. The blonder the better. We're tired of arroz con pollo. We want arroz con Anglo.

II.

Do you really think it's fertilizer we spread over your lawns? No it's ozone killer. That's right, the hole in the ozone layer can be traced directly back to us. Traffic jams, drug addiction, gingivitis—all our doing. We've conspired with the federal government to divert your taxes into our coffers. FICA now stands for Frijole Ingestion Cash Advance.

III.

We don't want your wives, we want Califas, Arizona, and, just for the hell of it, Iowa. Soon you will wake to the ruckus of reggaeton, the boom of banda, the clatter of millions of little brown feet invading your schools, wherein anyone caught learning English will be charged with treason and deported.

Illegals of all countries, Unite!

WHILE LATE CAPITALISM

[crammd-&-bangin-against-each-othr-in-a-dark-aluminm-box-they-drop-like-fleas-or-croak-standin-6-hrs-into-th-trip-a-mothr-drapes-her-limp-babys-serape-over-th-mans-head-it-nods-back-&-frth-with-each-bump-in-th-road-thank-god-th-corpse-doesnt-smell-warm-piss-&-shit-make-bodies-vomit-on-bodies-th-coyote-cant-unlock-th-trailr-door-a-womn-tries-to-scratch-a-hole-thru-th-wall-she-prays-some-phrase-or-word-some-idea-that-resists-translation-into-Englsh]

HUNGER STRIKE

Again they slept
with thunder in
their bellies.

MYKILLADOREHER

That Lucia broke the machine twice in one week was evidence enough. He also offered this—she's no longer automatic, her stitches are crooked and once another seamstress found Lucia's "lost" sewing patterns in the trash. The security guard half listened as Lucia gathered her things. Then the manager turned directly to her—what is it with you? We give you work, put money in your pocket. She put on her best disappointed face as they escorted her past rows of itchy throats, bowed heads, the refrain of needle through fabric.

Check Out Receipt

Harold Washington Library
Center

Wednesday, September 4,
2019 5:09:36 PM

Item: R0500725079
Title: My kill adore him
Due: 09/25/2019

Total items: 1

492

Every day Elena counts pig. A pageant of molded plastic rolling down the conveyor belt. The task: grab Miss Piggy, pull gown over snout, fasten two tiny buttons, grab another. With each doll, Elena's hands grow stiffer. Her feet grow heavy as the concrete below. Dolls spit at her, or maybe this is imagined, but the ache in her legs might be real. The supervisor brushes against her back when he patrols the floor. After standing for hours, the room begins to blur. Her mouth opens like an empty wallet as naked dolls march on.

What will settle in, what will rise from the lungs of girls who still burn weeks after detox treatment at a local clinic. Speak of headaches, blurred vision, diarrhea. How they suck air thick with sulfuric acid. Acetone working past unfiltered exhaust systems and through their livers. Most return to work despite doctors' orders. Back inside, the tin roof and their steady perspiration remind them they're still alive—together one breathing, burning machine.

Like Celia's pockets, there's nothing but lint here. Lint & dead machines. The sound of layoffs & profit margins. Yesterday this department droned an unsynchronized rhythm of coughing girls tethered to well-lubed motors. Row after row of pre-asthmatic lungs. Black hair buried under perpetual white. The decision was made across the border, he tells them. Nothing I can do about it. Sometimes Celia would imagine the whole place caught inside a tiny globe. Something she could pick up. Shake.

A perpetual conveyor, he patrols her mouth. The sound of unfiltered white. Breathing margins. The task: grab Elena's hands. Pull. Fasten. He also offered crooked patterns. Put money in her hair. That Lucia broke. Was evidence enough? Molded vision as a refrain. An empty wallet will rise. Speak. How they exhaust systems. Despite the blurred other, the ache might be real. Something she could pick up. Across the border, nothing I can imagine.

NOTES

"Men Watching Men": The self-professed place to "meet the T-girls of your dreams," El Gato Negro Bar is an independently owned bar/club in Chicago that caters to primarily Latin@ patrons. Straight men often come here on the down low to gaze at or pick up transgender women.

"The War on Poets Goes On": The poem's title comes from a line in Daniel Borzutzky's essay "Sharp Teeth of Death: An Essay on Poets and Their Poetics." The poem is for Daniel Borzutzky and Francisco Aragón.

"Amputee Etcetera": The poem is for the entire crew from the Recreation Room reading series in Chicago.

––––––––

Many thanks to all who have supported my work in both big and small ways and to those whose suggestions have helped some of these poems along: Lisa Alvarado, Katy Balma, María A. Beltrán-Vocal, Daniel Borzutzky, Catherine Bowman, Brenda Cárdenas, Steven Cordova, B. Douglas Cox, Kyle Dargan, Alex DeBonis, Irasema Gonzalez (Tianguis), Roberto Harrison, Shane Krupinski, CJ Laity, Francesco Levato, Heather Madden, Dan Manchester, Tinola Mayfield, María Meléndez, Mike Michalski, Aaron Michael

Morales, Charlie Newman, Ken Pascual, Emmy Pérez, Barbara Perry, Mike Puican, Michael Rowley, Maura Stanton, Erin Teegarden, Rich Villar, Ellen Wadey (The Guild Complex), Michael C. Watson (Wordslingers), David Wojahn, and Kevin Young—all of you have inspired me more than you probably know. Much love & respect. I especially thank Francisco Aragón (and Letras Latinas) for his early and ongoing support and for his tireless efforts to launch new voices. Respect, love and gratitude go out to Justin Petropoulos, my friend, my editor, my teacher—I take you with me every time I sit down to write. To Lauren Levato (www.laurenlevato.com), not only did you create the most amazing cover art (yeah, you did), your piece helped me figure out the book's title— thank you for your genius. A very special thanks to Martín Espada for empowering an entire generation of writers and for selecting this manuscript for the Montoya Prize. I am eternally grateful to Mom, Dad, and Nedda for believing in me long before anyone else and for guiding me through the dark. And finally, to Andrés Montoya, wherever you may be, thank you for gracing us with your lines.

ABOUT THE AUTHOR

Paul Martínez Pompa earned degrees from the University of Chicago and Indiana University, where he served as a poetry editor for *Indiana Review*. His chapbook *Pepper Spray* was published by Momotombo Press in 2006. He currently lives in Chicago and teaches at Triton College in River Grove, Illinois.